LEAVING MY
After the Journey
HOMELAND

My New Home
After Yemen

CRABTREE
PUBLISHING COMPANY
WWW.CRABTREEBOOKS.COM

Heather C. Hudak

Author: Heather C. Hudak

Editors: Sarah Eason, Harriet McGregor, and Janine Deschenes

Proofreader and indexer: Wendy Scavuzzo

Editorial director: Kathy Middleton

Design: Paul Myerscough and Jessica Moon

Cover design: Samara Parent

Photo research: Rachel Blount

**Production coordinator and
  Prepress technician:** Ken Wright

Print coordinator: Katherine Berti

Consultants: Hawa Sabriye and HaEun Kim, Centre for Refugee Studies,
  York University

Produced for Crabtree Publishing Company by Calcium Creative

Publisher's Note: The story presented in this book is a fictional account
based on extensive research of real-life accounts by refugees, with the aim
of reflecting the true experience of refugee children and their families.

Photo Credits:
t=Top, c=Center, b=Bottom, l= Left, r=Right

Inside: Flickr: Adam Jones: p. 4c; Shutterstock: Abeadev: p. 7tl; AndriyA:
p. 16t; Asanru: p. 13; Bumihills: p. 26t; Rob Crandall: pp. 19c, 24c;
Elenabsl: pp. 10t, 11r; Great Vector Elements: p. 11tr; Francisco
Sandoval Guate: p. 24b; Tatiana Gulyaeva: p. 25cr; Charles Harker:
p. 22t; Isovector: p. 19b; Helga Khorimarko: pp. 11tl, 18t; KittyVector:
p. 5t; Janos Levente: p. 15t; Light S: p. 23t; LineTale: p. 18c; Macrovector: p.
28b; Maxx-Studio: p. 4tl; Meunierd: pp. 6–7b, 22b; Mspoint: p. 28t; Byron
Ortiz: pp. 8c, 18b, 19t, 20, 21, 23c; Matyas Rehak: pp. 16–17b; Assaf Ben
Shoshan: p. 27; Ulrike Stein: p. 12; Sudowoodo: pp. 17b, 29t; Sunflowerr:
p. 4tr; SunshineVector: p. 3; Olivier Tabary: p. 26b; Shawn Talbot: p. 11c;
Tateyama: p. 16c; What's My Name: p. 15b; Murat Irfan Yalcin: p. 25b;
Zzveillust: p. 6tr; UNHCR: © UNHCR/Santiago Escobar-Jaramillo:
p. 10; © UNHCR/Tito Herrera: pp. 8–9b; © UNHCR/Betty Press: pp.
14–15b; © UNHCR/R. Ramirez: p. 28; © UNHCR/A. Serrano: pp. 14–15t;
© UNHCR/Daniele Volpe: pp. 6–7c; Wikimedia Commons: U.S. Army
photo by Sgt. Austin Berner: p. 29c.

Cover: Shutterstock: NonSense.

Library and Archives Canada Cataloguing in Publication

Hudak, Heather C., 1975-, author
    My new home after Yemen / Heather C. Hudak.

(Leaving my homeland : after the journey)
Includes index.
Issued in print and electronic formats.
ISBN 978-0-7787-4984-4 (hardcover).--
ISBN 978-0-7787-4990-5 (softcover).--ISBN 978-1-4271-2126-4 (HTML)

    1. Refugees--Yemen (Republic)--Juvenile literature. 2. Refugees-
-Ontario--Toronto--Juvenile literature. 3. Refugee children--Yemen
(Republic)--Juvenile literature. 4. Refugee children--Ontario--Toronto-
-Juvenile literature. 5. Refugees--Ontario--Toronto--Social conditions--
Juvenile literature. 6. Refugees--Social conditions--Juvenile literature. 7.
Yemen (Republic)--Social conditions--Juvenile literature. 8. Boat people--
Yemen (Republic)--Juvenile literature. 9. Boat people--Ontario--
Toronto--Juvenile literature. I. Title.

HV640.5.A6H833 2018   j305.9'06914095330713541   C2018-903017-8
                                                     C2018-903018-6

Library of Congress Cataloging-in-Publication Data

Names: Hudak, Heather C., 1975- author.
Title: My new home after Yemen / Heather C. Hudak.
Description: New York, New York : Crabtree Publishing, 2018. |
  Series: Leaving my homeland : after the journey | Includes index. |
Identifiers: LCCN 2018029946 (print) | LCCN 2018032291 (ebook) |
  ISBN 9781427121264 (Electronic) |
  ISBN 9780778749844 (hardcover) |
  ISBN 9780778749905 (pbk.)
Subjects: LCSH: Refugees--Yemen (Republic)--Juvenile literature. |
  Refugees--Canada--Juvenile literature. | Refugee children--Yemen
  (Republic)--Juvenile literature. | Refugee children--Canada--Juvenile
  literature. | Yemen (Republic)--History--Civil War, 2015---Juvenile
  literature. | Refugees--Social conditions--Juvenile literature.
Classification: LCC HV640.5.A6 (ebook) |
  LCC HV640.5.A6 H82 2018 (print) | DDC 953.305/3--dc23
LC record available at https://lccn.loc.gov/2018029946

Crabtree Publishing Company

www.crabtreebooks.com   1-800-387-7650

Printed in the U.S.A./092018/CG20180719

Published in Canada
Crabtree Publishing
616 Welland Ave.
St. Catharines, Ontario
L2M 5V6

Published in the United States
Crabtree Publishing
PMB 59051
350 Fifth Avenue, 59th Floor
New York, New York 10118

Published in the United Kingdom
Crabtree Publishing
Maritime House
Basin Road North, Hove
BN41 1WR

Published in Australia
Crabtree Publishing
3 Charles Street
Coburg North
VIC, 3058

What Is in This Book?

Sahar's Story: From Yemen to Canada

Hello! My name is Sahar, and I am a **refugee** from Yemen. When I was eight years old, my family fled the country. A **civil war** had broken out in 2015 and fighting spread across Yemen.

My family lived downtown in the Old City of Sana'a. Our apartment was hit by a bomb. My Mãmã was badly injured. My baby brother died. We had no place to live. We stayed with family while Mãmã was in the hospital. It was a scary time for my family.

My bãbã (father) did not think we were safe in Yemen once the war started. He said we had to leave as soon as Mãmã was out of the hospital. I was sad to go, but I knew it was for the best.

About 80 percent of Yemen's population under the age of 18 is in need of aid, such as food, shelter, or medical care.

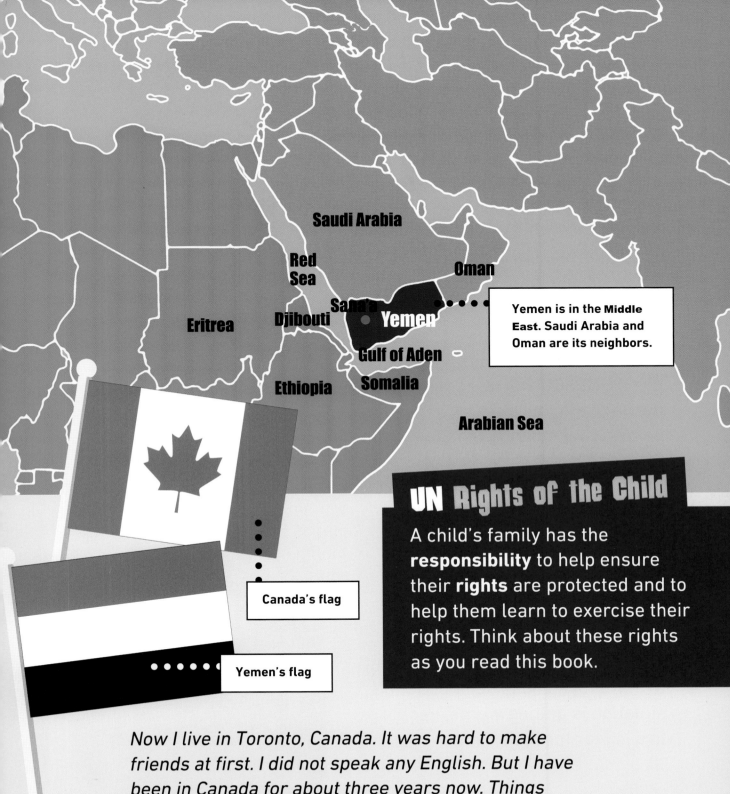

Saudi Arabia

Red
Sea

Oman

Sana'a

Eritrea

Djibouti

Yemen

Gulf of Aden

Ethiopia

Somalia

Arabian Sea

Yemen is in the **Middle East**. Saudi Arabia and Oman are its neighbors.

Canada's flag

Yemen's flag

UN Rights of the Child

A child's family has the **responsibility** to help ensure their **rights** are protected and to help them learn to exercise their rights. Think about these rights as you read this book.

Now I live in Toronto, Canada. It was hard to make friends at first. I did not speak any English. But I have been in Canada for about three years now. Things have changed a lot for me. I made many friends once I joined my school soccer team. I hang out with them on weekends. We like to ride our bikes and play video games. Now, I love it here!.

My Homeland, Yemen

Yemen is a country with a wonderful **culture**. It has a lot of fascinating cities. Sana'a is one of them. It is a **UNESCO world heritage site** because of its beautiful buildings made from earth and brick. Today, much of Sana'a looks very different. Many of the city's buildings have been destroyed by bombs. People live among garbage and ruins.

Some people stay in Yemen because they do not have enough money to leave. Others do not want to leave loved ones behind. But the situation is getting worse. People live in fear for their lives.

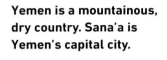

Sana'a

Yemen is a mountainous, dry country. Sana'a is Yemen's capital city.

Sana'a is home to more than 1.9 million people.

According to United Nations (UN) officials in 2017, the war has led to the world's worst **humanitarian crisis**. Millions of people are without homes, food to eat, or clean water to drink.

The war began in 2014. In the first three years of the war, there were more than 160,000 bombing attacks.

Diseases are making many people very sick. The country is having the biggest cholera outbreak in history. Nearly 8 million people are living in areas affected by this disease. It is spread by dirty water and food. Few people get the health care they need. Thousands of schools are closed. The electricity does not work 90 percent of the time.

Sahar's Story: Leaving My Homeland

It has been three years since we left Yemen, but I remember it like it was yesterday. After my house was bombed, I lived at my uncle's house with my sister and my mãmã. My bãbã and my brother were staying with friends. We did not live together as a family for months. I was scared every time I heard bombers fly over the city. I did not know if my bãbã and my brother were okay. I was relieved when Mãmã was well again.

It was dark outside when Mãmã woke me. I had no idea what was going on. I tried to ask, but Mãmã told me to be quiet so I would not wake anyone. Bãbã and my brother were waiting for us on the street. A **smuggler** took us in a big truck to Aden, Yemen. There, we got on a boat headed to Obock, Djibouti.

Nearly 40,000 Yemeni refugees have fled to Djibouti since 2015.

This is Markazi Camp in Djibouti. People living there are afraid of attacks by hyenas and wolves. Scorpions and snakes also enter their tents.

Yemen

Djibouti

Story in Numbers

About

956,000

Yemeni refugees have returned home to Yemen.

The boat ride was short, but very dangerous. The water was rough, and I was sick. People were crying all around me. No one wanted to leave Yemen. But we had to if we wanted a chance at a better life.

The refugee camp at Djibouti was very crowded. The heat was unbearable. There was not enough food and we worried about sandstorms destroying our tents. It was so horrible that many people left. Some returned to Yemen. Many months later, we were told we could go to Canada. My family was so happy to hear the news!

A New Life

Even if refugees are lucky enough to be given refuge in a new country, **resettling** there is not easy. Most live in refugee camps for months or years before they are sent to a **host country**. The **United Nations High Commissioner for Refugees (UNHCR)**, as well as some private organizations, help refugees find new homes.

Not all refugees who apply are approved. Refugees applying to live in many countries, such as Canada, must first be checked to make sure they can live there. First, the UNHCR interviews refugees to see if they are a good fit for the host country. If they pass the interview, they must undergo a health exam and security checks to make sure they are healthy and innocent of any serious crimes.

To be considered for resettlement, refugees must **register** with the UNHCR and governments.

To be considered a refugee, a person needs to be outside their homeland and have a fear of **persecution** there.

For adult and child refugees, settling in a new country such as Canada involves learning a whole new culture.

The Canadian government has many programs to help refugees adapt to life in their new country. Refugees can apply for a **loan** to pay for their travel costs to Canada. When they arrive, all government-helped refugees are given money to live on each month. It is meant to help with food, housing, and transportation.

Government support lasts for one year after refugees arrive in Canada, or until they can support themselves, whichever is first. Larger families or people with special needs may get more money.

UN Rights of the Child

The government has a responsibility to make sure your rights are protected. They must help your family to protect your rights and create an environment in which you can grow and reach your potential.

Sahar's Story: Arriving in Toronto

I was so excited to fly on an airplane! I never dreamed I would have the chance. There were other refugee families on the plane with us. We knew a little about Canada. We learned in school it is the second-largest country in the world in size. But we knew nothing about life in Canada.

When we were close to landing, I looked out the airplane window. All I could see was white snow. I had never seen snow before. It was so beautiful. It was also a reminder of how different from Yemen our new home would be.

Traveling by plane is often a new experience for child refugees.

More than 2.8 million people live in Toronto. It is the most-populated city in Canada and the fourth most-populated city in North America.

Dear cousin,
I am writing to you from the computer lab at my new school. You would love it here. I get to ride a bus to school every day. The library is filled with so many books! I cannot wait until I can read English better. Then I will read whatever I want.

Most of the kids are really nice here, but some days are still hard. It is difficult to make friends. I feel as though I am so different from everyone else here. This makes me feel lonely sometimes. I miss you so much. I wish you could be here safe with us.
Love,
Sahar

A woman named Amal met us at the airport when we landed. Her family came to Canada from Iraq when she was a child. She spoke to us in **Arabic**. We were so relieved. We did not speak any English.

Amal took us to our temporary home at a hotel. She told us the hotel would provide all our food and shelter for the next few weeks. Amal came back a few days later to see how we were doing. She told my parents about other programs to help refugees.

A New Home

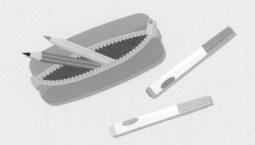

Most refugees have few, if any, belongings when they arrive in their new country. Many are forced to leave everything behind, and they need assistance when they arrive in their new country. They also need help adjusting to the culture of the new country. It is often very different from their homeland.

In most cases, refugees are given information about how to apply for health care, set up bank accounts, and register their children for school. But these activities can be stressful, especially when refugees are not English speakers. The Canadian government provides **counselors** to help refugees find a home. But there is a long wait. It can also take many months before refugees meet their counselor. Refugees often do not leave the hotel much during this time. Many do not speak English, so they cannot ask for help getting around or accessing services.

Eating fast food may seem ordinary to a Canadian child, but Yemeni children are not used to these types of food.

UN Rights of the Child

All adults should do what is best for you. When adults make decisions, they should think about how their decisions will affect children.

The government of Canada helps refugees with many things during their first year in Canada. The Resettlement Assistance Program helps pay for housing and school supplies for children. It helps pregnant women pay for any special care they may need. It provides money for families with babies to buy clothing and furniture.

Many communities have programs to help refugees get settled in their new home. Some, such as the YMCA, offer child care services, sports activities, and English language skills programs. Groups, such as Skills for Change, provide training in business skills and skilled trades so newcomers can get jobs in Canada.

The Canadian government supplies documents in Arabic and other languages. These can help refugee parents access important information such as health care options for their children.

Using new transportation systems such as the subway in Toronto can be a challenge for refugees when they first arrive in a host country.

Sahar's Story: My New Home

Amal did her best to help our family for the first few weeks we were in Canada. But there were some things she could not make better for us. We lived in the hotel for three months before we were given a counselor. It was so boring. I started to watch some TV, too. It helped me learn some English words.

I still jumped every time I heard an airplane going over. I got so scared a bomb was going to drop on us. I knew it was silly. Canada is very safe, but I could not help feeling that way.

Counseling helps refugees develop ways of coping after their very difficult experiences.

Story in Numbers

In 2017, Canada welcomed

403

refugees from Yemen.

We all missed my baby brother. Māmā cried a lot. Her legs were not the same as before the bombing and the surgeries she had afterward. She had a lot of pain. Amal found a doctor who could help Māmā get better. She got us all appointments to talk to a therapist who works with a lot of refugees. It is hard to talk about what happened.

Having a new home instead of a hotel room can help refugees feel a little more settled in their new life.

We finally found an apartment. But we needed chairs, beds, dishes, and a lot more. It was not easy setting up a new home. Luckily, there is a large Muslim community here. They have helped us get settled.

Bābā is looking for a job now. My parents worry about how we will manage when the government stops giving us money.

Cousin, my bābā got a smartphone today! I used it to film our new home in Toronto—I am taking you on a tour! As you can see, the building is very tall. We are on the eighth floor. Look how much space there is in the city! Can you see all of the parks? This is the elevator we ride to our apartment. Can you believe we do not have to take the stairs? This is my bedroom. I am so thankful for all the clothes in my closet and my toys. The camel is my favorite. It reminds me of the deserts in Yemen! How is everyone there in Yemen? Is there still fighting there?

17

A New School

Newcomers in Canada must register their children in school. The school meets the family and child to decide which grade level is best for the child.

Some refugee children are behind other students in Canada. They may have not had the chance to go to school for a while. Other students may show special skills in certain subject areas, such as math or science. The school helps find the best classroom and programs for each child.

In Canada, the law in most provinces states that children must attend school until they are at least 16 years old.

Programs such as the Bridge to Teaching program encourage teachers from across the world to come and teach in Canadian schools. The teachers are often able to communicate with refugee children in their own language. They may even have been refugees themselves.

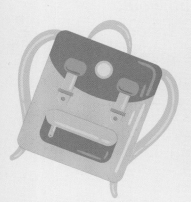

Schools in Alberta, Canada, offer Arabic language classes so other students can also learn the language. Schools may also arrange for translators to attend school events, such as parent-teacher meetings.

Some refugee children suffer **trauma** due to their experience. Many schools are beginning to offer counseling to help them cope. Some schools also have settlement workers to help refugee and **immigrant** children adjust to their new school.

Most schools have after-school programs, such as arts and science clubs and sports teams. These programs can be a good way for newcomers to make friends. They can also help children learn more about Canadian ways of life. School visits to museums, workplaces, and other places can help children learn about Canada's history and culture.

UN Rights of the Child

You have the right to a good quality education. You should be encouraged to go to school to the highest level you can.

Sahar's Story: A New Way of Learning

I was so scared to start school. Amal brought me some of her daughter's jeans and T-shirts so I would fit in with the other kids. In Yemen, I walked to school. In Toronto, my school is too far away to walk. I catch the school bus at the corner of my street. Mãmã walked with me to the bus stop for the first week to be sure I got there okay.

Traveling to school in Canada is a new experience for some refugee children—especially during snowy winters!

Story in Numbers

Between 2005 and 2014,

150,000

refugees and their children or elderly relatives became permanent residents of Canada.

My teacher is very nice. She told me which desk to sit at. A girl named Emily said she would show me around the school. It is huge! There are so many classrooms. It is strange to have boys in my class. In Yemen, the boys went to a different school.

I was shy at first. I only spoke a bit of English, so I did not want to talk. Emily was very nice. She introduced me to her friends. I was so scared I would not fit in. That is when I met Fatima. She is Muslim like me. She helped me talk to the other children. Kids at my school come from all over the world. I am already feeling comfortable at school.

Physical education in Canadian schools is very different from Yemeni schools. Refugee children have to get used to new sports and being taught in a new way.

Hi Aaliyah, Sadeeqaty (my friend)! I got a tablet! It is mainly for my schoolwork. But I can use it to take videos, too. This is the first entry in my new video diary! Today, we are on a field trip at the Fort York National Historic Site. The fort was built about 200 years ago. The people here think it is very old, can you believe it? I showed them pictures on the Internet of Sana'a and told them how Yemen is thousands of years old. I am learning so much about Toronto's history and people. I hope we go on more trips like this! Got to go now. Bye.

Everything Changes

Provinces, cities, and towns in Canada have different programs to assist refugees. In bigger cities, there may be many groups and services. In smaller towns, there may only be one or two places where refugees can find support.

Many other organizations help make sure newcomers feel welcome in Canada. The Arab Community Centre of Toronto helps families of all backgrounds and cultures from the moment they arrive in Canada. They help them build new lives by giving them help with everything from finding a house to getting a driver's license. They also have youth camps and education programs.

These people are welcoming refugees to Canada at Toronto's Pearson International Airport.

Small towns in Canada can be less expensive for refugees to live in. However, larger cities have more physical spaces where newcomers can connect with each other and make friends.

The Youth Network is the young people's division of the Canadian Council for Refugees. They hold discussions, conferences, and workshops to help newcomers face challenges in their new home.

Some Canadians take part in special events and activities to help welcome newcomers to the country. Schools sometimes hold fundraisers in support of refugees. They may pack gift bags to give out when refugees arrive at the airport or hold up handmade signs welcoming the refugees to the country.

Some choirs learn songs in other languages, such as Arabic, to sing at events celebrating the arrival of new Canadians. These are just a few of the ways Canadians help refugees feel at home in their new country.

UN Rights of the Child

You have the right to choose your own friends and join or set up groups, as long as they are not harmful to others.

Sahar's Story: My New Way of Life

One of the first things we did when we got to Toronto was find a mosque we could go to. We met so many other refugee and immigrant families there. Many of them came to Canada with nothing but the clothes on their backs. They knew what it was like to try to build a new life. We often go to their houses for dinner. They even showed us where to shop for Yemeni foods.

Muslim food must be halal, or prepared in a special way according to Islamic law.

One of our new friends helped my bãbã find work. A warehouse was looking for someone to stock shelves. The manager who hired him spoke Arabic. It made the job interview easier for Bãbã. We are so thankful for our new community. We do not know how we would have gotten by without its help.

Many Muslim families enjoy a large feast at the end of Ramadan, the Islamic holy month of fasting.

Fatima's cousin has been helping me learn to write in English. It is so hard to remember the right letters, but I am getting better at it each day. My friends like learning about my culture, too. One night, Mãmã helped me make a huge Yemeni meal. We invited Emily and a few other kids from school. It was so much fun!

Dear cousin,
I went to my friend Emily's house for a sleepover this weekend. When we woke up, the Easter bunny had hidden chocolate eggs all over the house. We had to hunt for them. I loved it! After, we went to her church. I learned about Easter and Lent. I learned that Lent is a time for prayer and giving back to the community. Ramadan is a time for prayer and giving, too!
I will write you again soon.
Sahar

Sahar's Story: Looking to the Future

For the most part, life in Canada is good. It was difficult at first to adjust to life in a new country. The winter was so cold, and I hated the food. But my family has come a long way over the past three years. My brother and sister barely remember Yemen. I tell them stories and show them pictures. I do not want them to forget where we came from.

I now speak English as well as I speak Arabic. I got top grades in all my classes this year, too. I want to make my family proud.

Lawyers help refugee families exercise their rights. They may help them apply for **asylum** and reunite families that have been separated.

UN Rights of the Child

You have the right to find out things and share what you think with others, by talking, drawing, writing, or in any other way unless it harms or offends other people.

Each year, more than 130 refugees study at Canadian colleges and universities.

My mãmã is pregnant with a new baby. It will be a Canadian **citizen**—the first in our family! We all hope to become Canadian citizens one day. We have to be here for six years first. Then we must take a special test to show we know about Canada's language and history.

My bãbã takes classes three nights a week. He wants to work as an engineer again, like he used to in Yemen. His training back home was not up to Canadian standards. It may take a few years before he has completed the courses he needs.

Dear cousin,
I heard you are coming to join us! I am so excited! I've missed you all so much. When do you think you will get here? I guess it could still be a long time. Write and tell me soon!

I have lots of news. I joined the soccer team at school. It is an all-girls' team. We practice after school and on weekends. I hope to get a **scholarship** so I can go to university when I finish high school. I want to become a lawyer. Then I can help refugee families like mine. Back in Yemen, because of the war, I would never have dreamed of such an opportunity.
Sahar

Do Not Forget Our Stories!

Many refugees face a long, tough journey to get to another country. They may live in refugee camps for months or even years. When they arrive in their host country, they often need to complete a lot of paperwork and adapt to very different ways of life. In many cases, they will never be able to return to their homeland. The situation in Yemen is getting worse each day.

Not all people are friendly to refugees. Sometimes refugees experience **racism** or hatred of their religion. Refugees have the right to feel safe and welcome in Canada. They have the same rights as other Canadians when it comes to getting health care, finding work, going to school, and more.

Organizations such as the Canadian Council for Refugees (CCR) help make sure refugees' rights are protected. CCR makes sure refugees are treated fairly in the workplace and in school. They ensure refugee children are well cared for and try to make sure refugees do not experience racism.

It is up to each of us to support and stand up for people of all backgrounds and cultures.

Refugees and immigrants have helped shape Canada. They have helped add diversity to their communities by sharing their art, foods, and music. Refugees who work contribute to their new countries by paying **taxes** to the government. Many are doctors, nurses, and teachers. They create programs to help others and are important parts of their communities.

It is important that people try to help refugees in any way they can—just as it is important not to forget their stories. We should also notice how Yemeni refugees and immigrants are building great communities in their host countries. They are creating positive futures for themselves and their families after their difficult journeys from their homelands.

Discussion Prompts

1. How are Yemeni refugees important parts of their new communities?
2. What would be the hardest part of starting over in a new country for you?
3. What types of support are available for refugees in Canada?

Glossary

Arabic A language spoken in the Middle East and North Africa

asylum Protection given to refugees by a country

citizen A member of a country who has the rights of that country

civil war A war between groups of people in the same country

counselors Professionals who offer guidance about personal problems

culture The shared beliefs, values, customs, traditions, arts, and ways of life of a group of people

host country A country that offers to give refugees a home

humanitarian crisis An event that brings harm to the health, safety, and well-being of a large group of people

immigrant A person who voluntarily leaves one country to live in another

loan Money that can be borrowed and paid back later

Middle East Countries in southwestern Asia and northern Africa that stretch from Libya to Afghanistan

persecution Cruel treatment

racism The belief that some races of people are not equal to others

refugee A person who flees from his or her own country to another due to unsafe conditions

register To be officially recorded

resettling Settling in a new or different place

responsibility The duty to deal with something

rights Privileges and freedoms protected by law

scholarship A special payment made to support education

smuggler A person who moves people or things illegally

taxes An amount of money paid to a government for services, such as education

trauma A very severe shock or very upsetting experience

UNESCO world heritage site A landmark or area that is protected by law because of its historic or scientific importance

United Nations High Commissioner for Refugees (UNHCR) A program that protects and supports refugees everywhere

Learning More

Books

Howell, Sara. *Refugees* (The American Mosaic: Immigration Today). PowerKids Press, 2014.

O'Neal, Claire. *We Visit Yemen* (Your Land and My Land: The Middle East). Mitchell Lane Publishers, 2011.

Roberts, Ceri. *Refugees and Migrants* (Children in our World). Barron's Educational Series, 2017.

Websites

http://ccrweb.ca/en/youth/welcome
Find out more about the youth division of the Canadian Council for Refugees by watching this video.

www.unhcr.org/yemen-emergency.html
Get the facts about the humanitarian crisis in Yemen.

www.unicef.org/rightsite/files/uncrcchilldfriendlylanguage.pdf
Explore the United Nations Convention on the Rights of the Child.

Index

About the Author

Heather C. Hudak travels all over the world and loves to learn about different cultures. She has been to more than 50 countries, from Brazil to Indonesia and many others in between. When she is not on the road, she enjoys spending time with her dog named Mouse and cat named Turtle.